D0796810

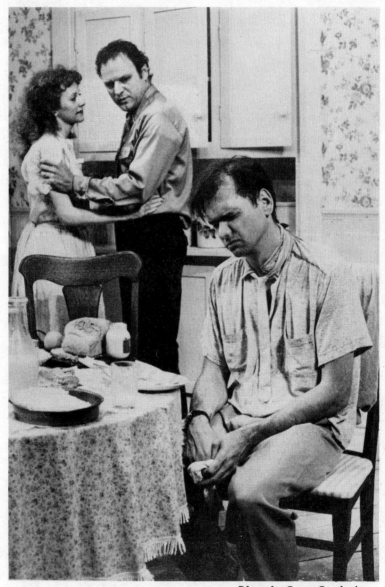

Photo by Gerry Goodstein

Jessie K. Jones, Bill Smitrovich and Murphy Guyer in a scene from The People's Light and Theatre Company production of "The American Century."

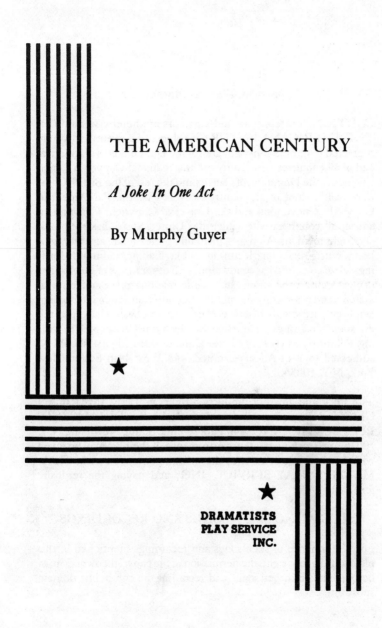

THE AMERICAN CENTURY

A Joke In One Act

By Murphy Guyer

DRAMATISTS
PLAY SERVICE
INC.

THE AMERICAN CENTURY was originally presented at the People's Light and Theatre Company in June, 1984. It was directed by Steve Abrizzi, the set design was by Norm Dodge, the costume design was by Megan Frechter. The cast was as follows:

WOMAN .... Jessie Jones

MAN .... Bill Smitrovich

STRANGER .... Murphy Guyer

THE AMERICAN CENTURY was commissioned by and subsequently produced at Actors Theatre of Louisville.

THE AMERICAN CENTURY

The time is the Spring of 1945. The place, an American kitchen. It is spacious, bright, and cheerfully decorated. The comforting pastels of a Norman Rockwell illustration. Among the furnishings is a table with four chairs, and a cathedral radio. As the lights fade to black, we hear the final bars of Tommy Dorsey's rendition of "On The Sunny Side Of The Street."* In darkness, the mild, resonant voice of a 'forties disc jockey comes from the radio.

RADIO. "Leave your worries on the doorstep. Life's sweet. On the sunny side of the street." ..... That it is ..... Mister Thomas Dorsey and his orchestra ..... This hour of music dedicated to the boys on the boats. Yes girls, they're coming home. Soon they'll be walking down Main Street just as we remembered them. Let's sprinkle those memories with a little stardust, shall we. Artie Shaw. *(The Artie Shaw version of "Stardust" plays. * Lights rise on a woman washing dishes at the sink. Sunlight streams in through the window above it. She is a pretty woman in her mid-twenties. She works efficiently and thoroughly, but her mind is obviously elsewhere. ..... A door closes offstage...... After a pause the woman calls out, more from habit than interest.*

WOMAN. Mother? *(A moment later a man appears. He too is in his mid-twenties. He wears an army uniform and a cap. He carries a duffel bag. He stands quietly and watches the woman from behind. Pause. Unaware of his presence and still preoccupied with her thoughts, the woman calls out again.)* Mother, what are you doing back so early?..... *(The woman freezes. A sudden realization sweeps over her. She knows that someone is standing behind her, and although she has not seen him in four years, she knows intuitively who it is. The dish slides from her hand. A moment later she turns. They stand apart and look at each other*

---

*See Special Note on copyright page.

5

for a long silent moment. Without taking his eyes off her, the man slowly drops his duffel bag and removes his cap. She runs into his arms. An everlasting embrace. Finally she speaks.) Is it you? Is it really you?

MAN. It's really me.

WOMAN. Oh Tom. Oh God, Tom.

MAN. Shhhh. It's all right.

WOMAN. Hold me. Hold me before I faint.

MAN. I've got you.

WOMAN. Oh Tom.

MAN. It's all right, it's all right.

WOMAN. I knew it was you. I just knew it. I don't know how but I did. I was afraid to look. I was afraid that if I turned around, you'd be gone!

MAN. I'm right here.

WOMAN. Like in my dreams. I'd try to touch you in my dreams and you'd disappear... But you're really here.

MAN. I'm really here.

WOMAN. And it's not a dream? Tell me it's not a dream.

MAN. It's not a dream.

WOMAN. Oh God, I've waited for this for so long.

MAN. So have I.

WOMAN. I was so frightened.

MAN. I know, I know.

WOMAN. I kept telling myself that if I could just make it through one more day. But so many days. So many years. Oh Tom, don't ever leave me again.

MAN. I won't.

WOMAN. Promise! Promise me you won't ever leave again!

MAN. I promise, I promise. Now come on, stop crying. I'm back. And I'm here to stay.

WOMAN. I love you so much.

MAN. And I love you.

WOMAN. *(Pulling away abruptly.)* Oh my God, are you all right?! You're not hurt are you?!

MAN. No, no, I'm fine.

WOMAN. Are you sure?! They didn't hurt you, did they? You

weren't injured or—

MAN. I'm fine, I'm fine. Everything's fine.

WOMAN. It's not fine! You had me worried half to death! Why didn't you write?! Why didn't you call me and let me know you—

MAN. I couldn't. We didn't have time.

WOMAN. I thought something had happened to you! I thought something terrible had—why didn't you tell me you were coming?!

MAN. I didn't have the chance.

WOMAN. Well it's not fair! Look at me! I'm a mess!

MAN. You're not a mess.

WOMAN. My hair is dirty, my face, this old rag dress.

MAN. It doesn't matter.

WOMAN. How could you do this to me?! It's not fair!

MAN. Margaret.

WOMAN. I had it all planned. I had new stockings and lipstick.

MAN. Margaret it doesn't matter! ... I don't care about your stockings. Or your lipstick. I care about you. The way you are.

WOMAN. I'm old.

MAN. No you're not.

WOMAN. When you left I was young and pretty, and now I'm old and ugly.

MAN. You're even more beautiful than I remembered you.

WOMAN. You're just saying that.

MAN. And I'd love you even if you weren't. *(She embraces him.)*

WOMAN. Oh Tom I'm sorry. I'm acting like a spoiled schoolgirl.

MAN. I understand.

WOMAN. I just wanted everything to be perfect that's all.

MAN. It is perfect.

WOMAN. I guess I'm just so used to worrying.

MAN. Well you can stop now. It's over.

WOMAN. ...It is, isn't it? It's really over.

7

MAN. It's really over.

WOMAN. ... What was it like? Was it awful?

MAN. Sometimes ... I don't know, I don't want to talk about it. It's done, it's finished, it's not important anymore. What's important is us. I want to talk about us. Margaret, listen, sit down, I have to tell you something.

WOMAN. What is it? Did something happen?

MAN. Oh I'll say something happened.

WOMAN. What?

MAN. ... Ready?

WOMAN. What?! What?!

MAN. I got a job ... Yeah! Can you believe it?!

WOMAN. But, but when, how, how did—

MAN. One of the guys from my squad is the vice president of a bank over in Fairview. He promised to have a job waiting for me when I hit stateside. A good one too. He said that they were looking for guys like me. He said that with a service record like mine the opportunities were unlimited!

WOMAN. Tom that's wonderful!

MAN. And that's not all. Wait till you hear this. He said he knew of a house for us... Yeah. About twenty miles from here. He said it's a bit run down right now but that with a little work it'd be just perfect. It's got a garden in the front, with two acres of land in the back, and it's got three floors.

WOMAN. Three floors?

MAN. With bedrooms on every floor!

WOMAN. But, but how will we be able to afford it?

MAN. It's all taken care of. The government is giving out these special loans to G.I.'s who want to buy homes but don't have the down payment. My application is already in. Everything's set. And listen to this. This is the best part of all. Every month I've been putting aside a little bit of my pay. You know, so we'd have something to get started with. Anyway it added up to over five hundred dollars.

WOMAN. Five hundred?

MAN. And on the boat coming back? I got into this poker game

8

with a bunch of C.O.'s and—

WOMAN. Oh Tom you didn't lose it?!

MAN. Lose it? I doubled it! I drew to an inside straight and I won! One thousand dollars!

WOMAN. A thousand dollars?!

MAN. A thousand bucks! A thousand smackers! And it's all ours baby. Free and clear ... We're in clover Margaret. We're on our way. All those years of scraping pennies to make the rent? ... Of looking for work that was never there? ... Of worrying about where our next meal was coming from? ... They're gone. They're all over. We're going to have a big house and a big car, everything we always wanted.

WOMAN. Everything?

MAN. Enough to keep you in stockings and lipstick for the rest of your life.

WOMAN. I can hardly believe it.

MAN. Believe it Margaret. It's true.

WOMAN. Our very own house?

MAN. just waiting for us to move in.

WOMAN. How many bedrooms does it *have?*

MAN. I don't know. Five? Six?

WOMAN. Six?!

MAN. *(Pointedly.)* Is that too many?

WOMAN. *(Blushing.)* ... No.

MAN. We're going to have that big family Margaret. We're going to have kids playing and laughing in every corner of that house.

WOMAN. Oh Tom!

MAN. And we're going to give those kids everything we never had. The best schools, the best doctors.

WOMAN. And the first one will be a boy.

MAN. Yeah. And he'll be strong and healthy.

WOMAN. And smart and handsome.

MAN. A ballplayer. Another Duke Snyder.

WOMAN. Or a doctor. Like Albert Schweitzer.

MAN. Or a banker, like his old man.

WOMAN. And you can take him with you when you go fishing?

MAN. Yeah, and I'll take him out to Ebbets Field.

WOMAN. And to the Circus. And we can take the whole family on trips up to Mountain Lake.

MAN. Sure! We'll get our own little summer cottage.

WOMAN. What do you mean? You mean *buy* one?!

MAN. I'm going to be a banker. I'll just give myself a loan.

WOMAN. You're terrible! *(They laugh.)*

MAN. Margaret from here on out it's going to be nothing but the best. I know it's hard to believe, but it's true .... You know, when we were driving through those small towns in France, I don't know, you should've seen it. The streets were jammed with people. Hanging from the street lamps. Leaning out the windows. And they were all cheering, and screaming, and waving American flags. And the women were holding up their kids for us to kiss. And this one kid grabbed me and held me around the neck, and I looked into his eyes and, I don't know. I don't know how to explain it. I just felt that somehow it had all been worth it. It's a new world Margaret... It's a whole new ballgame. That's what I felt when that kid hugged me. I felt like anything was possible. Like there wasn't anything we couldn't do, anything we couldn't have, once we put our minds to it. And it's all out there. Just waiting for us to grab it. A life more wonderful than we ever dreamed was possible ... We made it Margaret. We're home. *(Tommy Dorsey's "Getting Sentimental Over You" is playing on the radio.*) May I have this dance? (They approach each other tenderly. Smiling through tears, they gaze into each other's eyes. Transported by a happiness they had never dared to imagine, they dance .... Lights dim ... The quintessential image of America's fondest memory..... They dance. Suddenly we become aware of another presence in the room. A Stranger ... A man in his thirties. He is slack jawed, seedy and slovenly dressed in clothing that is definitely of the period but somewhat exaggerated. He wears a camera around his neck. He watches the couple dance with a look of gaping astonishment.)*

STRANGER. Oh my God. *(He begins to take his camera out of it's case. The Man and the Woman stop dancing. They turn slowly and stare at the intruder. The stranger is having trouble with the camera case.)*

---

*See special note on copyright page.

10

MAN. Who's he?

WOMAN. I don't know.

MAN. You don't know?

WOMAN. He does look familiar.

STRANGER. *(Talking to a stubborn snap.)* Come-aaaaan.

MAN. All right Margaret, who is this guy?

WOMAN. I have no idea.

MAN. Then how did he get in here?

WOMAN. I don't know, stop snapping at me.

MAN. I'm not snapping at you, I just want to know who he is.

WOMAN. Well, I'm sure I haven't got the vaguest notion.

MAN. *(Turning off the radio.)* Hey, you! What the hell are you doing here?

WOMAN. Tom.

MAN. What?

WOMAN. Watch your language.

MAN. Well who is he?

STRANGER. Who, me?

MAN. Yeah, you.

STRANGER. Uh, nobody. I'm nobody. I'm not here. Look, just go on with—

MAN. What do you mean you're not here? You're standing in my kitchen. You think I'm blind?

WOMAN. Mother's kitchen.

MAN. What?

WOMAN. This is Mother's kitchen.

STRANGER. Oh right. I thought it looked familiar.

WOMAN. Have you been here before?

STRANGER. Just to visit. I recognized the doilies. And the smell.

MAN. Who are you anyway?

STRANGER. It's that baking smell.

MAN. How did you get in here?

STRANGER. Smells like cake or pie or something.

MAN. What do you want?

STRANGER. *(Peering in the breadbox.)* Wow, homemade bread.

11

MAN. What the hell is going on here?!

WOMAN. Tom! Mind your tongue.

MAN. Margaret for godsake, a complete stranger is wandering around our house.

WOMAN. It's Mother's house. And I'm sure there's a perfectly reasonable explanation.

STRANGER. Hey, great radio.

MAN. I'd like to hear it.

STRANGER. Me too. How do you turn it on.

WOMAN. He must be one of Mother's salesman friends. They like to drop by for coffee and cake.

MAN. Hey you.

STRANGER. *(With his ear to the radio.)* Great.

MAN. We don't want any. Now turn that thing off and get the hell out.

WOMAN. Tom!

MAN. What?

WOMAN. What is wrong with you? Show a little common courtesy for heaven's sake. Where are your manners?

MAN. Manners?

WOMAN. You're being belligerent.

MAN. I just got back from the war.

WOMAN. That's no excuse to be rude ... If you can't keep a civil tongue in your head then don't bother opening your mouth.

STRANGER. God, look at these tubes.

WOMAN. Excuse me.

STRANGER. They're enormous.

WOMAN. Excuse me?

STRANGER. Hey do you guys get Jack Benny on this thing?

WOMAN. Well yes. On Sunday. Why, do you like Jack Benny?

STRANGER. Oh yeah, he's my favorite.

WOMAN. Really? Mine too.

STRANGER. Yeah, he's great isn't he?

WOMAN. I listen to him every week.

STRANGER. Yeah, and Don, and Dennis, and Rochester.

WOMAN. And Mary Livingston, and Maxwell the car?

STRANGER. "This is a stick up. Your money or your life."
(Woman plays along and takes the pause.) "Well?"

WOMAN. "I'm thinking, I'm thinking." *(They laugh together.)*

STRANGER. Great, great.

MAN. Margaret.

WOMAN. ... Oh, yes. Look, uh, Mister...?

STRANGER. Oh call me Tom.

WOMAN. Really? My husband's name is Tom. His name is Tom
too Tom. Tom too. Two Toms. Isn't that funny.

MAN. *(Flatly.)* Hysterical.

WOMAN. Yes, well.... tell me Tom, just what is it that you
sell?

STRANGER. Sell?

WOMAN. Aren't you a salesman?

STRANGER. No. I mean sometimes I do a little selling part-
time, between semesters. But that's not why I'm here.

WOMAN. It's not?

MAN. Then why the hell *are* you here?

WOMAN. Tom! Please!

MAN. Margaret, for godsake, we haven't seen each other in
four years.

WOMAN. Well if we've waited this long I don't think another
minute is going to kill us. Now control yourself ... Now Tom, tell
me, if you're not here to sell us anything, then what exactly are you
here for?

STRANGER. Well ..... Well I'm really *not.* I mean not *really.*

WOMAN. You're really not what?

STRANGER. Well... Well I *am,* I mean obviously I *am.* Kind of.
I guess.

WOMAN. You are what?

STRANGER. All right, look, first of all, this is not how it was supposed to be, all right? Nobody said anything about a confrontation.
I mean I'm as shocked by this as you are. And it's not at all what I
was expecting. I mean *I* was figuring on some cheap old motel. You
know, some dusty joint that rented by the hour. Or some

13

junkyard Chevy with worn upholstery. Or maybe even a movie theatre. You know, some dive that was showing old newsreels for thirty five cents that—

MAN. *What do you want?!!!*

STRANGER. —I want to see my conception. *(Pause.)*

MAN. What?

STRANGER. I know, I know, it's crazy! But it's part of my therapy.

WOMAN. Therapy?

STRANGER. Yeah. You see my analyst is this Neo-Freudian Geneticist. And he believes that the Oedipal conflict originates in the pre-consciousness of genetic memory. Steinfranck says that the only way to get to the bottom of my pathological narcissim is to trace it back to my pre-fetal experience.... He calls it fertilization trauma ... Frankly I'm pretty skeptical of the whole idea ... But what am I supposed to do? I've tried just about every kind of therapy there is. I've been through primal, behavioral, confrontational ... I've tried EST, acupuncture, modern dance. None of them worked. So I figured I had nothing to lose.

WOMAN. Are you not well?

STRANGER. Are you kidding? I'm not even close. I've been going through this bout of depression you wouldn't believe. I mean in six years I can only remember being happy *once.* And I think that was just a chemical imbalance.

WOMAN. But what's wrong? What is it?

STRANGER. Borderline Schizophrenia.

WOMAN. Oh dear. Is that what you have?

STRANGER. Yeah. All my friends have it too. Listen, do you think that maybe I could have a glass of water?

MAN. No.

WOMAN. Of course. Let me get it for you.

MAN. Margaret!

WOMAN. Tom, for heaven's sake, have a little compassion. Can't you see that he's ill. Look, he wants to take his medicine.

STRANGER. Anti-depressants. They're not much help though. I think I've developed a resistance.

MAN. I'll say he's ill. He's nuts. *(Sotto voce.)* What

14

does he mean he wants to see his conception?

WOMAN. ..... Yes, what *did* you mean by that?

STRANGER. It's Steinfranck's idea. He thinks it might trigger some primal response that could lead to a cure. God I hope he's right. The holidays are coming up.

MAN. Who are you anyway?

STRANGER. Tommy.

MAN. Tommy who?

STRANGER. Tommy Kilroy, your son.

MAN. That does it. *(The Man crosses to his duffel bag and begins searching through it.)*

WOMAN. But we don't have a son.

STRANGER. Well no, not yet. But you will.

WOMAN. We will?

STRANGER. The first of December.

WOMAN. But how can that be?

STRANGER. I was three weeks early.

WOMAN. But it just doesn't seem possible.

STRANGER. Oh it is. It's inevitable.

WOMAN. My future son here today?

STRANGER. Well the first one anyway.

WOMAN. I can hardly believe it.

MAN. Of course not. It's bullshit.

WOMAN. It's miraculous.

MAN. It's ridiculous.

WOMAN. Our son!

MAN. What son?!

WOMAN. Didn't you hear what he just said Tom?

STRANGER. Hey we got anything to eat Mom?

MAN. We don't have a son. Remember?

WOMAN. No but we *will!* In December!

MAN. The hell you say!

STRANGER. *(Peering in the ice box.)* I haven't eaten all day.

WOMAN. And he's come all this way just to see us!

MAN. Get a grip on yourself Margaret, Jesus.

STRANGER. Any spiced ham, or baloney?

15

MAN. It's a sham. This guy's a phony!

WOMAN. He's our baby, come for a visit!

MAN. He's crazy. Don't be an idiot!

STRANGER. Any cheese spread?

MAN. *(Brandishing a gun.)* You! Drop that bread!

WOMAN. Tom!

STRANGER. Mom!

MAN. Drop it!

WOMAN. Stop it! ... Thomas Kilroy you put that down!

MAN. Margaret he's stealing our food.

WOMAN. It's mother's food. And you put down that Luger this instant!

MAN. Margaret for godsake!

WOMAN. You might be able to get away with that kind of behavior in the army, but not here! I will not tolerate gunplay in my mother's kitchen. Now give me that thing before someone gets hurt ..... Come on?!

MAN. *(He hands it over reluctantly.)* I want him out of here. *(She removes the clip, drops it into her apron, and tosses the gun in the trash.)*

WOMAN. Tommy you go right ahead and eat whatever you like.

MAN. What!

STRANGER. Thanks Mom.

MAN. Margaret are you out of your mind? What are you doing? Are you crazy?

WOMAN. No I am not crazy? Now calm down and get a hold of yourself.

STRANGER. Yeah Dad, don't be a jerk.

MAN. Don't call me that.

WOMAN. Tommy don't call your father a jerk.

MAN. No, *Dad!* Don't call me Dad!

STRANGER. Hey we got any mayonnaise Mom?

MAN. And stop calling her Mom!

WOMAN. I'll get it honey.

MAN. And don't call him honey! Margaret for godsake, you can't mean to tell me you actually believe all this horseshit?

WOMAN. Tom, please! Not in front of the k-i-d.

MAN. What k-i-d? He's older than I am. And we don't have any k-i-dees, remember?

WOMAN. No, but we will.

MAN. Yeah. In the future.

WOMAN. Well that's where he's from.

MAN. From the *future?*

WOMAN. Why not?

MAN. Because it's impossible.

WOMAN. Why?

MAN. Because .... how did he get here?

STRANGER. Drugs.

WOMAN. Tom, you just said it yourself. You just said that it was a whole new world. That anything was possible.

MAN. But not this. Not this for chrissake. This is ridiculous. It's perposterous. It's inconceivable.

STRANGER. I wish you wouldn't put it like that.

MAN. Margaret, I'm telling you, this guy is a freeloader. He's a vagrant, a bum.

WOMAN. Well that may be, but he's still our son.

MAN. How can you say that? You never even laid eyes on him before.

WOMAN. A mother always knows.

MAN. I don't believe this is happening.

WOMAN. Tommy stop that, you're making a mess.

MAN. Margaret for godsakes, think about what you're saying. Just stop and take a minute and think about it. It just doesn't make any sense, don't you see?

WOMAN. Not everything in this world makes sense Tom.

STRANGER. Good point Mom.

WOMAN. There are many things in this life that we don't understand. And we'll probably never understand them. We just have to accept them on faith,

STRANGER. Yeah, like quarks.

WOMAN. ....Quarks?

17

STRANGER. Sub-atomic particles.

WOMAN. Oh ...

STRANGER. Yeah and black holes, and white drawfs, and super-novas. Or what about telekinesis? Or Cybernetics? Or Civil Defense? I mean who knows whether these things actually even exist? Not me. I don't understand any of it. I mean the day Buzz Aldrin stuck a flag in the moon that was it for me. Things have gotten just too complicated.

MAN and WOMAN. The moon?

STRANGER. Oh yeah. We put men on the moon. Don't ask me how.

MAN. Who did?

STRANGER. We did. The United States.

WOMAN. The United States of America put men on the moon?!

STRANGER. Yeah. The Sea of Tranquility. It was weird. They played golf.

WOMAN. Golf?

STRANGER. Yeah. They hit this tee shot? Went like ten miles. Hey Mom we got any mustard?

WOMAN. Spicy or regular?

MAN. Wait a second, wait a second! Just hold on one minute here. Let me get this straight. Are you telling me that the United States of America took a guy named *Buzz*, sent him all the way to the *moon*, and that when he got there he played *golf* on an *ocean* and hit a *ten mile tee shot?????* Is that what you're telling me?

WOMAN. Was there a tournament?

STRANGER. The Sea of Tranquility isn't an ocean, it's a desert. And it's not like they went up there just to play golf. That would be stupid.

WOMAN. *(Taking Tommy's side.)* Of course it would.

STRANGER. Nobody's going to spend billions of dollars to send some guy millions of miles into space just so he can work on his golf game.

WOMAN. Certainly not.

MAN. So what *did* they go up there for?

18

STRANGER. Rocks.

WOMAN. Rocks?

STRANGER. Moonrocks.

MAN. I'm calling the police.

WOMAN. Tom!

MAN. Moonrocks my foot.

WOMAN. You would call the police on you own son?!

STRANGER. Wouldn't be the first time.

WOMAN. Tom! How can you?!

MAN. No Margaret, don't bother defending him. I don't know who this character is, but he is *not* my son. He's nothing but a two-bit con artist. Don't you see what he's trying to do? He's trying to turn you against me. Well I'm not going to let him get away with it. Now I want this lazy, sponging good-for-nothing out of my house and I want him out now!

STRANGER. Oh wow, deja-vu.

WOMAN. It's not your house. And I will not allow you to throw our son out on the street.

MAN. He's not our son! Look at him for chrissake. He doesn't even look like us.

STRANGER. ..... Everybody always used to say I looked like Uncle Phil.

WOMAN. Why yes, of course. No wonder he looked familiar. Look Tom, he looks just like my brother Phil. See? Around the eyes?

MAN. All right, all right, fine! I'm going to put an end to this crap right now. You say you're our son, right? Right. And you say you believe him? Fine ... Prove it.

STRANGER. What do you want, a bloodtest?

MAN. Don't tempt me.

WOMAN. Prove it how?

MAN. Well if he really is our son he must know a lot about us. Right?

STRANGER. Oh I get it. You want background. All right, all right. Let's see. You were both born and raised in Schenectady, New York. Mom has six brothers and sister, and you have three.

19

WOMAN. Right!

MAN. Public record stuff.

STRANGER. .... When you were a kid? You had to walk five miles without shoes to get to school every day.

MAN. Wrong! It was only six blocks! Ah hah!

STRANGER. ... Figures.

MAN. There, see? What did I tell you?

WOMAN. You told *me* it was twelve blocks.

MAN. ..... Go on.

STRANGER. You met Mom in high school, but you didn't start going together until your senior year. Mom didn't like you at first because your hair tonic smelled like fish oil. She didn't want to be seen with a guy all her friends called tunahead.

WOMAN. That's true! That's absolutely true! .... Sorry.

MAN. Tunahead?

WOMAN. Well it stunk Tom.

MAN. It was the same hair tonic Gable used. I didn't hear you calling him tunahead.

WOMAN. Well *I* never called you that.

MAN. Who was it? ..... Phyllis?

WOMAN. What difference does it make? The point is he got it right.

MAN. It was Phyllis, wasn't it?

WOMAN. What else?

MAN. Was it Phyllis?

WOMAN. What else?

STRANGER. When you enlisted in the army you made friends with four guys. Two of them, Tony Pancotti and Butch Conklin, were captured. In ... Tunisia. Manny Eisenblatt contracted venereal disease in Algiers. And the fourth one, Benny Bellows, faked amnesia after he fell out of a jeep at Anzio and ran away with a nurse he met at the hospital in Palermo!

WOMAN. *(Astonished.)* Is that right?

MAN. Lucky guess.

WOMAN. Then it's true! He *is* our son!

STRANGER. Can we get on with this thing now. My session only

20

lasts forty five minutes.

WOMAN. Oh Tom isn't it wonderful? We're going to have a son. A son named after you. A son you can take fishing.

STRANGER. Fishing?!

WOMAN. You don't like fishing?

STRANGER. I hate fishing.

WOMAN. Oh ... Well what about the circus? You like the circus don't you?

STRANGER. Not really.

WOMAN. Well how about baseball? You must like baseball!

STRANGER. Nah. Competition makes me anxious. I mean what's the point? When you lose you feel lousy, and when you win it's only good for a couple of minutes. And you can't even enjoy those couple of minutes because all you can think about is how lousy you're gonna feel when they're over.

MAN. ..... What *do* you like?

STRANGER. I don't know. I like some things. Movies. I like cable TV. I guess I'm kind of visual.

MAN. My God.

WOMAN. Do you have any brothers and sisters?

STRANGER. Oh yeah, four of them.

WOMAN. Four?! Do you hear that Tom? Four brothers and sisters. Five children. The big family we always dreamed of.

STRANGER. Yeah, and all by caesarean.

WOMAN. What?

STRANGER. I know. Can you believe it?

WOMAN. All of them?

STRANGER. Yeah. And the only one who was under ten pounds was Tim. And he turned out to be gay.

MAN. What?

STRANGER. Yeah. But he's still in the closet so don't tell him that I told you.

WOMAN. What?!

STRANGER. Look, it's no big deal all right. It's just the way he is.

21

WOMAN. But how long has he been—

STRANGER. All his life. He says he always felt that way. Since he was thirteen.

WOMAN. Thirteen!

STRANGER. Believe me Ma, it was obvious. I don't know how you missed it.

WOMAN. And he won't come out?

STRANGER. He's afraid to. He's afraid he might lose his job. Look Ma, don't worry about it. He's fine, really. He's just real sensitive that's all.

WOMAN. *(Searching for the bright side.)* Well, as long as he's gay.

STRANGER. Exactly.

WOMAN. What about the others? What are their names?

STRANGER. Well you got me, Timmy, Billy, Suzie, and Jenny.

WOMAN. Oh yes, of course. Mother's name is Jenny.

STRANGER. Yeah Jenny was born just after Mom-Mom died.

WOMAN. Oh no, Mama died?

STRANGER. Yeah, what a relief. She had Alzheimer's disease. Her mind just fell apart. It got so bad, the whole family had to start wearing name-tags around the house. Finally Dad put her in a nursing home in the Bronx. About a year later she died of botulism.

WOMAN. Tom!

MAN. What?

WOMAN. You put my mother in a home?!

MAN. No!

WOMAN. How could you?!

MAN. I never did!

STRANGER. Don't lie, you did too.

MAN. I didn't! I wouldn't!

STRANGER. Yes you will. You always hated Mom-Mom... You know what he used to do? He used to—

MAN. Why you little—

STRANGER. Mom!

22

WOMAN. Tom!

MAN. I'll kill him! I'm going to kill him!

WOMAN. You'll do nothing of the kind! Now you put him down. You hear me?! Put him down this instant..............Now try and get along why can't you?

MAN. Get along with a liar?

STRANGER. It's true

MAN. It's a lie!

STRANGER. True!

MAN. Lie!

STRANGER. True!

WOMAN. It doesn't matter! ... Now stop your bickering, both of you. We'll just have to cross that bridge when we come to it. There's nothing we can do about it now at any rate so I don't want to hear another word about it ... I want to hear about my children. And what they're doing with themselves in the future.

STRANGER. Not much. Collecting unemployment mostly.

WOMAN. Tommy, you mentioned something about semesters. Are you going to some kind of school?

STRANGER. Yeah, college.

WOMAN. College?! Well my goodness. Do you hear that Tom? Your son is going to college. Isn't *that* exciting!

STRANGER. Not really. After eleven years it gets to be pretty predictable.

MAN. Eleven years?

WOMAN. Good Lord, what are you studying?

STRANGER. Well at first I wasn't studying much of anything. It just seemed so irrelevant you know? I mean how could I sit in some boring history class when history was actually being made right outside the window. I mean people were dying in the streets. It was time to get involved, ya know? To join the struggle against oppression. To wage war against injustice and ignorance ... I mean we were the Armies of the Night!

WOMAN. So you quit school?

STRANGER. Well, no. I didn't want to lose my draft deferment ... Besides, I was getting college credit toward my Political

23

Science course.

WOMAN. You're studying to be a political scientist?

STRANGER. Nah. After Watergate I got disgusted with the whole political process. It's just too corrupt. And to tell you the truth, the women in the department were real unattractive. Besides, it was just about then that the economy got bad. So I decided I'd better get serious and learn how to do something. I mean I didn't want to end up like one of those guys with grey pony-tails who live in their Volkswagons. So anyway, I figured I'd go into pre-med.

WOMAN. A doctor!

STRANGER. Well, no. After a couple of years I had to quit. Turned out they had a language requirement. What a pain. They wanted me to *memorize* Greek. So I switched majors and decided to study law instead.

WOMAN. Well that's good.

STRANGER. Are you kidding? Those people are totally amoral! I couldn't believe it. I mean you're not even supposed to ask the guy if he's guilty. They don't care about justice. All they care about is winning. I'm telling you, flunking that bar exam was the best thing that ever happened to me. Really woke me up. After that I went through this intense period of of self-evaluation. And I suddenly realized that I had this real problematic relationship with money. It was almost puritannical. I mean there's nothing wrong with making money. Right? As long as you don't get too compulsive about it. So I went into business administration. But that didn't work out either. I don't know, I just don't seem to have a head for numbers. And then after that there was Communication, and then Sociology, and then Psychology and then finally I said the hell with it. I'll be a writer. I mean that's what I always wanted to do anyway. It's like I've got all these stories that really need to be told, ya know?

WOMAN. So you're going to be a writer?

STRANGER. Nah. I failed the course.

MAN. Oh my God.

WOMAN. So what will you do now?

STRANGER. God, I don't know. I guess I'll have to take that job with the government. I mean it's either that or be a banker.

MAN. What's wrong with being a banker?

STRANGER. It's boring.

MAN. It's work. Work is work. If it was all fun and games they wouldn't pay you to do it. Wise up kid. Get a job. Stop freeloading.

STRANGER. Oh look, don't start in on me, all right. I've had a rough trip.

MAN. You don't get anything in the world for nothing Pal. Life is damn hard. And the only way you're going to get anywhere in it is by work. By the sweat of your brow. You won't get it by laying around some fancy ass college.

WOMAN. But Tom, you were just saying how you wanted all your children to have an education?

MAN. Well I didn't realize they were going to make a career out of it.

WOMAN. Well, yes, eleven years does seem an awful long time. My goodness Tommy, how did you manage? That must have cost an awful lot of money.

STRANGER. Oh yeah, and don't think I didn't appreciate it.

MAN. What?

STRANGER. Hey Mom we got anything for dessert?

WOMAN. You haven't finsihed you sandwich.

MAN. Wait a minute.

STRANGER. Yes I did.

WOMAN. What about that crust?

MAN. Wait a minute.

STRANGER. Aw Mom, crust is boring.

MAN. Margaret, did you hear what he just said?

WOMAN. Let me handle this Tom. Now you listen to me young man. There are children in India who have never even *seen* a crust of bread. And if you think—

STRANGER. Not anymore, not anymore. The United States went in with money and advisors and taught them how to irrigate. India's a food *exporter* now.

WOMAN. You mean there are no more starving children?

STRANGER. Well, there's still the Third World.

WOMAN. The Third World?

STRANGER. Yeah, you know. Africa, Jamaica, Mississippi.

MAN. The hell with the Third World!

WOMAN. Tom! Shame on you!

STRANGER. Dad's right. People are sick of hearing about it. I mean what more can we do?

WOMAN. We can finsih our crust.

STRANGER. Then can I have dessert?

WOMAN. There's lemon meringue pie in the icebox.

MAN. Margaret didn't you hear what he said?! He spent eleven years in college and stuck *us* with the bill!

STRANGER. Relax Dad. I was only enrolled for nine. After Billy's accident I had to go to California for a couple of years to get my head together.

WOMAN. Billy's accident?

MAN. Who paid for *that?*

STRANGER. Yeah, all right, but what about those two years I took off to knock around Europe? That didn't cost you anything. Unless you're gonna count that bail money for those trumped up drug charges in Amsterdam.

WOMAN. Our son Billy?

MAN. Bail money?

STRANGER. It was a plant. I was framed.

WOMAN. What happened?

MAN. And what did *that* cost me?

STRANGER. I don't know, what's the big deal, it's only money.

MAN. Only money?! Did you hear that?! Only money he says! What do you think, you think money grows on trees?! I'll give you "only money!" When I was ten years old I had to sell newspapers on the street to put food on the table. My eight year old brother was shining shoes at the train station!

STRANGER. Oh God, spare me the boring depression stories.

WOMAN. What kind of accident?

MAN. Boring de—did you hear what he just said?!

STRANGER. Look, if you didn't want to spend money, you shouldn't have had kids.

MAN. Well if you think I'm going to have *you,* you got another think coming!

STRANGER. Hey I didn't ask to be born ya know.

MAN. Yeah? Well we can take care of that right now.

STRANGER. Mom!

WOMAN. Tom! Stop it! Stop it I said. Take you hands off him. Take them off this instant! ..... *(He does so.)* ..... And keep them off. And Tommy you stop provoking your father.

STRANGER. He started it.

WOMAN. I don't care who started it. I just want it stopped. We are supposed to be a family. And it would be nice if just once we could try and act like one ..... Now I want to know what happened to Billy.

STRANGER. Great, my camera is broken.

WOMAN. You said he had an accident.

STRANGER. Yeah, he blew up.

WOMAN. What?

STRANGER. Well after he got back from Vietnam, he turned into this anti-war radical. And—

WOMAN. Vietnam?

STRANGER. That's in Southeast Asia. And—

WOMAN. What was he doing there?

STRANGER. Oh God, who knows. Anyway, he was making this bomb for a local peace organization and it accidently went off.

WOMAN. Oh my God, he's not dead is he?

STRANGER. Well no.

WOMAN. Oh thank God.

STRANGER. Not exactly.

WOMAN. ..... Not exactly?

STRANGER. Well he's kind of in a coma.

WOMAN. Oh no.

STRANGER. Yeah, he's been in it for years. It's been a real strain too. I mean the only reason he's still breathing is because they've got him hooked up to this artificial life machine. You wouldn't believe how much that stuff costs.

MAN. How much?

STRANGER. Oh thousands.

MAN. Oh my God.

STRANGER. But they say there's still brain activity so nobody can decide what to do.

MAN. Let him die.

WOMAN. Tom!

STRANGER. Dying's not as easy as it used to be Dad. Except for poor people.

WOMAN. You are talking about your son!

STRANGER. Still, it is pretty depressing. You and Suzie are the only ones who still visit him. You know, to cut his hair and trim his nails? But even Suzie's getting a little fed up. If she had her way they'd pull the plug and we'd all sit around and chant.

WOMAN. Chant?

STRANGER. Yeah. Suzie's into religion. She got into it after her abortion.

MAN. Abortion!

STRANGER. Yeah. At first she was involved with this love cult that was run by this Korean arms manufacturer. But she quit that after you guys kidnapped her and had her deprogrammed. And then she was a Charismatic Catholic for a while. But I guess that was just too exhausting. And then last year she moved into an ashram and became an anorexic.

WOMAN. She's living in an ashcan?

STRANGER. No, ash*ram.* It's this place where people go to meditate and empty their minds so that they can be one with the universe.

WOMAN. Is it in outer space?

STRANGER. .... No. It's on Fourteenth Street.

MAN. What's an anorexic?

STRANGER. That's a woman who punishes her parents by starving herself to death.

WOMAN. Why would she want to punish us?

STRANGER. Hates ya I guess.

WOMAN. But why?

STRANGER. I don't know. Maybe you made her feel insecure or something.

WOMAN. How did we do that?

STRANGER. I don't know, look, I wouldn't get too hung up about it. All kids hate their parents.

MAN. Since when?

STRANGER. Since the early sixites.

WOMAN. This is terrible.

MAN. It's a nightmare.

STRANGER. Great pie Mom.

WOMAN. What about Jenny?

STRANGER. *(Reluctantly.)* ... Yeah.

MAN. Yeah what?

STRANGER. Yeah, she hates you too.

WOMAN. But why?!

STRANGER. Well she doesn't exactly hate *you.* Just what you stand for, that's all.

WOMAN. What I stand for?

STRANGER. *(Guiltily.)* Jenny says you're a male imperialist stooge..... She says that your compulsive cleaning is just a symptom of the guilt you feel about wasting your life in mindless servitude.

WOMAN. ..... I don't understand.

STRANGER. Hey me neither. Sounds paradoxical if you ask me.

WOMAN. But what happened? What did I do?

STRANGER. Nothing. I mean you did the best you could Ma. Really. It's just that raising kids nowadays is almost impossible.

WOMAN. Do *you* have children?

STRANGER. Nah. I had a vasectomy. It was my wife's idea. Carol said it wasn't fair that it was always the woman who had to be responsible for birth control. I could see her point.

WOMAN. So you're married.

STRANGER. Divorced. When she turned thirty Carol panicked and decided she wanted to have kids afterall. So she left me.

WOMAN. That's awful.

STRANGER. Yeah. But I guess she had to. It was a matter of self actualiztion.

WOMAN. But now you can't have children.

STRANGER. Oh I don't know. I could always adopt a refugee or something. There's always plenty of those around.

WOMAN. What's happened to all my children?

STRANGER. Yeah. Pretty messed up bunch, huh? But it's really not our fault. I mean you have to remember, we were the first generation to grow up with the Bomb. You can't imagine what that's like. I mean do you have any idea what it's like to live like that? That to live knowing that you and everybody around you could be blown up at any second?!

MAN. Yeah.

STRANGER. ... Yeah, but do you know what it's like to live in a world where a single madman could bring all of civilization to the brink of destruction?!

MAN. Yeah.

STRANGER. ... Yeah, but do you know what it's like to be young and idealistic, and to spend years fighting for peace and justice, and then to find out that none of it made any difference?!

MAN. I'm beginning to.

STRANGER. It's different with my generation.

WOMAN. Why?

STRANGER. Because *we* were different.

MAN. How?

STRANGER. We were special.

WOMAN. Why?

STRANGER. Because we were.

MAN. How?

STRANGER. Because, we were non-conformists!

WOMAN. Who was?

STRANGER. Everybody! *(Confused pause.)*

MAN. What?

STRANGER. Yeah, well you guys were pretty obnoxious too! Thought you were the last word just because you won a war ... I mean give us reasons like you guys had and even we could've been war heroes. Hitler, Mussolini, Pearl Harbor! God, you guys got all the breaks.

MAN. I give up.

WOMAN. But my own children hating me.

STRANGER. Oh it's not that bad, Ma. They don't hate you now. I mean once you got old and fat it just seemed cruel to—

WOMAN. Fat!

STRANGER. Oh, yeah. After all the kids grew up and left home, you got real depressed. Menopause I guess. Anyway, you got addicted to diet pills. Dad had to pack you off to a de-tox center. You got better. But when you came home all you seemed to want to do was eat. Which is perfectly understandable. I mean by that time Dad's drinking had gotten totally out of hand.

WOMAN. That's ridiculous. Tom doesn't drink. Why he's never even— *(She turns to see Tom opening a pint of whisky he removed from his duffel bag a moment before. He smiles sheepishly.)*

STRANGER. He's fallen off the wagon like ten times. After the fire he just stopped trying. Now he buys it wholesale.

WOMAN. What fire?

STRANGER. Oh, a few years ago Dad torched the house to collect the insurance.

WOMAN. Our house?

STRANGER. Yeah. He fell way behind on his gambling debts.

WOMAN. Gambling debts!

STRANGER. And then they started that audit at the bank so he had to hurry up and put back all the cash he embezzled.

WOMAN. Tom!

MAN. What?

WOMAN. You stole money from the bank to gamble with? How could you?

STRANGER. Oh no, that wasn't for gambling. He wanted that money to invest in that lodge up at the lake.

WOMAN. Our cottage at the lake!

STRANGER. Ten cottages.

31

WOMAN. Ten cottages?

STRANGER. Yeah. Dad was going to rent them out during the fishing season and make a bundle. But then the gas shortage hit and everybody stopped taking vacations. And right after that most of the fish got wiped out by acid rain. So he was stuck. He tried to torch that too, but he got caught. Probably would've done time if he hadn't filed for bankruptcy. Judge felt sorry for him.

MAN. Bankruptcy?

STRANGER. Yeah. That and Mom's cancer. *(He winces over letting that one slip out.)*

WOMAN. Stop it! Stop it! That's enough! I don't want to hear anymore. I can't. It's too awful. *(Pause.)*

STRANGER. Look maybe I shouldn't have said anything.

WOMAN. But what about the good times? Weren't there any of those? There must have been good times too.

STRANGER. Oh sure, sure.

WOMAN. Well tell us about those. Tell us about the good times. *(Long pause.)* Well?

STRANGER. I'm thinking, I'm thinking.

WOMAN. This is dreadful.

STRANGER. Oh there were the reunions.

WOMAN. Reunions?

STRANGER. Yeah. Every year you and Dad go to the reunion of Dad's old batallion. They have parties, and banquets, and you all get drunk and talk about the good old days.

MAN. The good old days?

STRANGER. Yeah, you know, the war, the depression... You guys really look forward to it.

WOMAN. This is horrible.

MAN. I need a drink.

WOMAN. My own daughter hating me, my son in a closet, my house burned to the ground..... No.... No, I don't believe it! It's not true. It can't be true.

STRANGER. I wish it weren't.

WOMAN. It isn't! I know it isn't! I refuse to believe that. It's just not possible.

MAN. It's no use, Margaret.

WOMAN. What?

MAN. It's no use. It's a losing hand.

WOMAN. What are you saying?

MAN. We crapped out.

WOMAN. Thomas Kilroy, you stop that! I won't permit that kind of talk!

MAN. It's true. What's the use in pretending.

WOMAN. It's not true! Sure, maybe a few things will go wrong, maybe it won't turn out exactly like we planned, but no matter what happens, no matter what lies ahead, there's always hope.

MAN. I don't see it, Margaret.

WOMAN. Tom, we love each other. That's what's important. That's all that matters. And as long as we have that, we can face anything. We can. You know we can.

STRANGER. Hey Mom.

WOMAN. I mean we've made it through bad times before, right? And we'll make it through again. The way we always have. Together.

STRANGER. Hey Mom, look, I'm eating my pie crust.

WOMAN. Two people who care for each other, and help one another. And besides, now that we know all these things, we'll be able to change it. It doesn't have to end up like this, don't you see? It'll be different now that we know.

STRANGER. *(Intentionally spills his milk.)* Hey Mom, I spilled my milk.

WOMAN. *(Oblivious to her son.)* Tom, we're just starting out. We can't quit now. Not now when we have a chance to change it. We have to at least try.

MAN. You're right, Margaret. You're absolutely right. We *do* have to try. And we *can* change it. We just have to want to, that's all. I mean forewarned is forearmed, right?

STRANGER. Not really.

MAN. Shut up, you ... I mean what are we talking about here? We're talking about our life, right?

WOMAN. Right.

MAN. And what happens to us in our life is up to us. It's up to *us* to decide. I mean, our destiny is in *our* hands.

WOMAN. Yes, yes.

MAN. Margaret, I give you my word. From now on, no more alcohol and no more gambling. I'll never touch another drink or place another bet as long as I live.

STRANGER. Yeah, sure.

MAN. I told you to shut it. Now shut it... You're right Margaret. It doesn't have to turn out this way. And we're going to prove it. We're going to show what people can do when they just accept a little personal responsibility. It won't be easy. But we can do it.

WOMAN. We can. I know we can. *(They embrace.)*

MAN. I don't know how all this could've happened. But this much I do know. It wasn't because these things *had* to happen. I mean it wasn't fate that was to blame. It was ourselves.

STRANGER. You always blamed it on the Dodgers.

MAN. What?

STRANGER. You used to say it all started when the Dodgers moved out of Brooklyn.

MAN. .... The Dodgers moved out of Brooklyn?

STRANGER. Yeah.

MAN. .... When?

STRANGER. 1958. O'Malley packed up the whole team and moved them to Los Angeles. They're the Los Angeles Dodgers now. *(Tom stares at Tommy for a long moment, and then dashes to his duffel bag and puts on his cap.)*

WOMAN. Tom, what are you doing?

MAN. It's no use, Margaret. It's a stacked deck. Sure, maybe I *could* quit drinking. And I might even be able to quit gambling. Maybe. But the Dodgers leaving Brooklyn?! What could I possibly do about that? Tell me Margaret. Tell me! What?!

WOMAN. You could write them a letter.

MAN. Goodbye Margaret.

WOMAN. Where are you going?

MAN. To re-enlist. *(He exits.)*

WOMAN. But Tom... Tom, wait!... Tom? He's gone.... He's

34

left me.

STRANGER. Ma, believe me, it's the best thing that ever happened to you.

WOMAN. But I waited for him for four years.

STRANGER. Yeah, while he was having a good time liberating Paris.

WOMAN. And now he's gone. *(She weeps.)*

STRANGER. ... Aw, aw Mom, don't cry.

WOMAN. All our plans. All our dreams.

STRANGER. Aw come on Ma. He's not worth it.

WOMAN. He was my husband.

STRANGER. But he was a creep.

WOMAN. And now I'm all alone.

STRANGER. .... You still have me.

WOMAN. .... You?

STRANGER. Why not? He never loved you as much as I did.

WOMAN. He didn't?

STRANGER. God no... I mean who was the one who never forgot your birthday?... Who was it that stood up to him when he got drunk and started yelling at you?... Who lied for you when you didn't want him to find out about that money you lost at Bingo?

WOMAN. Who?

STRANGER. Me. It was always me. He didn't care. God, all he cared about were interest rates and point spreads. I'm the one who was always there for you. I'm the one you always confided in.

WOMAN. Really?

STRANGER. Sure.

WOMAN. Do you really love me, Tommy?

STRANGER. Ma, you're all I ever wanted..... I mean I'm sure you've probably got serious reservations... I mean I know I didn't turn out exactly like you expected. And I wouldn't blame you if you were a little disappointed. But it's not all my fault. Really. It's not. You don't know what it's like in the future. You don't know what's going on back there. It's not even funny. It's terrifying. And the

35

worst part is that people pretend that it isn't. I mean no wonder I'm such a wreck... But it'll be different now. Now that I'm back here where it's safe I'll be able to change. And I will. Honest.

WOMAN. But Tommy—

STRANGER. No, I will. I promise. I'll, I'll be vigorous, and desisive. I'll be self assured again. Like I was when I was a kid. Because for the first time in twenty years I feel like, like I could really do something. Like maybe it's not so pointless after all. I mean maybe there really *are* answers!

WOMAN. But Tom is gone.

STRANGER. Forget him! Who needs him?! Don't you see, Ma? It's a whole new ballgame! A clean slate! I'll get it right this time! I will!

WOMAN. But he's your father.

STRANGER. Ma, please! Please don't make me go back there. It's too awful. There's no future back there! I'd rather die.

WOMAN. But if you don't have a father—

STRANGER. No! I mean it! I'd rather die! I'd rather be dead than have to go back to ...... what?

WOMAN. Well ... everyone has to have a father. Don't they?

(Long pause.)

STRANGER. Which way?

WOMAN. Left.

STRANGER. *(Running out the door.)* DAD? .... DAD I WAS JUST KIDDING! .... COME ON DAD, CAN'T YOU TAKE A JOKE?!

BLACKOUT

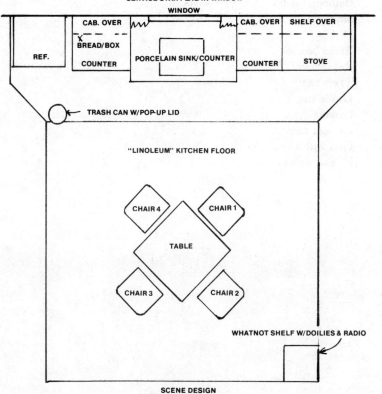

SCENE DESIGN
"THE AMERICAN CENTURY"
(Designed by Paul Owen for the Actor's Theatre of Louisville)

PROPERTY LIST

Table
Four chairs
Cathedral radio
Sink
Dishes
Bread box
Refrigerator
Trash can
Duffle bag
Camera
Camera case
Gun with clip
Pint of whisky

COSTUME LIST

WOMAN
> Yellow cotton 40's dress
> Apron with large pocket
> White socks
> Shoes

MAN
> Army — 1st Division/under Bradley
> Boots
> Hat

STRANGER
> 40's Salvation Army pants/green fatigues
> Old Hawaiian shirt
> Cap
> Overcoat
> Running shoes/sandals/old moccasins

New

PLAYS

THE DINING ROOM

THE WEST SIDE WALTZ

**THE LIFE AND ADVENTURES
OF NICHOLAS NICKLEBY**

SOMETHING CLOUDY, SOMETHING CLEAR

THE HOTEL PLAY

FRANKENSTEIN

THREADS

DARK RIDE

ELEGY FOR A LADY

TITANIC

AM I BLUE

THE UNDEFEATED RHUMBA CHAMP

DRAMATISTS PLAY SERVICE, INC.
440 PARK AVENUE SOUTH   NEW YORK, N.Y. 10016

NEW
Plays

'NIGHT, MOTHER
WHAT I DID LAST SUMMER
FEEDLOT
A DIFFERENT MOON
DOMESTIC ISSUES
DADDIES
THE HOUSE OF SLEEPING BEAUTIES
WIN/LOSE/DRAW
SLACKS AND TOPS
THE ART OF SELF-DEFENSE
TIME FRAMED
FLIGHT LINES & CROSSINGS

DRAMATISTS PLAY SERVICE, INC.
440 PARK AVENUE SOUTH   **NEW YORK, N.Y. 10016**

RECENT

 *Releases* . . .

MONDAY AFTER THE MIRACLE

STANDING ON MY KNEES

THE DAY THEY SHOT
JOHN LENNEN

THE MAGENTA MOTH

GOING TO SEE THE ELEPHANT

FAMILY DEVOTIONS

THE HABITUAL ACCEPTANCE
OF THE NEAR ENOUGH

GRANDMA DUCK IS DEAD

SCOOTER THOMAS MAKES IT
TO THE TOP OF THE WORLD

SILVER LININGS

MANY HAPPY RETURNS &
FAST WOMEN

24 HOURS AM & PM

Write for information as to
availability

DRAMATISTS PLAY SERVICE, Inc.
440 Park Avenue South   New York, N. Y. 10016

New
TITLES

FOOL FOR LOVE
DOG EAT DOG
MR. & MRS.
A PLACE ON THE MAGDALENA FLATS
COURTSHIP
MY UNCLE SAM
GREAT EXPECTATIONS
THREE SISTERS
TWAIN PLUS TWAIN
LAUGHING STOCK
BONJOUR LA BONJOUR
THE OMELET MURDER CASE

New

 # PLAYS

BABY WITH THE BATHWATER
THE LADY AND THE CLARINET
THE VAMPIRES
THE BEARD
LUNATIC AND LOVER
LITTLE BIRD
THE WHALES OF AUGUST
THE FATHER
THE SOUND OF A VOICE
POTHOLES
LES BELLES SOEURS
LITTLE VICTORIES

INQUIRIES INVITED

 DRAMATISTS PLAY SERVICE, INC.
440 Park Avenue South   New York, N. Y. 10016